STRIVE for Job Search Success

Doug Thorpe

ISBN: 0998107257

ISBN-13: 978-0-9981072-5-7 (HeadwayExec)

DEDICATION

This book is dedicated to those who are faced with finding a new job. The markets change almost daily. Having the right tools to land that next job are critical to your success. With my STRIVE model, I've seen thousands of job seekers find and win the right job at the right time.

You need your own edge. Get going with STRIVE.

"There can be no joy in living without joy in work." – Thomas Aquinas

And by the way, some of this going to sound like psychological counseling. It's NOT. This is practical advice from someone who has been in the deep end of high unemployment and some of the tightest job markets we've known in our lifetime.

Disclaimer – The materials and information presented here are not a substitute for professional psychological counseling. If your situation needs further help, seek the services of a licensed professional counselor.

TABLE OF CONTENTS

INTRODUCTION

SETTING THE STAGE

The year was 2009. The country was in the middle of the worst financial recession anyone could remember. Unemployment was at an all-time high, double digit numbers.

There were networking events springing up everywhere in town. People who had lost jobs were gathering to learn SOMETHING about where to go and what to do to find work.

At many of these gatherings, well-meaning so-called experts were "teaching" how to write resumes and how to perform during an interview.

One would think that would be helpful. So many of the people who just lost their job had never really had to search for a job. Therefore, writing a good resume was important, right?

Yet after weeks and months of using the standard teachings, few were finding work.

I was in this group. Yes, I had lost *my* job. Well really, I had lost my company.

My wife and I owned a mortgage services outfit that helped banks and lenders get through all their back-office paperwork. We had 200 companies coast to coast who relied on us for services.

Things were pretty good.....

.... until the crash.

Some of you may recall the first tidal wave that caused the financial crash was a meltdown in the mortgage market. If you had a business related in any way to mortgages, you had front row seats at ground zero of the nuclear blast.

Our company lost 75% of our business in just 45 days. Nothing was coming back for a long time.

I knew that because I called every owner/president of every institution we had as clients. I had hard talks with them about their view ahead. It was bad.

Sixty days later we made the painful decision to close the company.

There I was. No company. No job. No idea what I should do.

So, yes, I was looking at what to do. It made sense to participate in these networking events. But after a few months listening to the ideas, I just knew there was something more.

The New Organization and Better Ideas

My entrepreneurial juices were still flowing. I rallied some friends and contacts who were also trying to help job seekers.

We organized a new program named Jobs Ministry Southwest. It was a non-denominational, faith-based organization dedicated to helping job seekers.

In a very short period, we were hosting over 250 people per week attending our radical and disruptive programs for job search success.

I say radical and disruptive because we began teaching guerrilla tactics for job search.

The first thing we did was abolished the standard two-page long form resume. We introduced a shorter, punchier mostly single page resume. The heartbeat of this form was something called the Accomplishments Worksheet or Inventory.

I must pause to pay special recognition to long-time friend and partner in crime, Rick Gillis (Gillis, 2010) (RickGillis.com) for introducing me to this powerful solution.

The Process

The next thing I wanted to tackle was the whole job search process. For almost a year I had watched hundreds of desperate people slog through the old-school job-hunting techniques with little or no success.

The routine went something like this.

1. Write a resume which contained a listing of prior job history, boringly written to nth detail.
2. Go cold calling and door knocking dropping off the cookie-cutter copies of the written obituary, *err* I mean resume.
3. Wait…… for a long time
4. Send some emails
5. Go to more networking events (where, by the way, NO hiring managers ever showed up to)
6. Rinse and repeat

THAT was the process. Maybe one out of every 50 resumes got noticed. Maybe...

I just knew there had to be a better process.

I started asking more detailed questions of the people attending my events. Soon, several very large themes emerged.

These themes were undeniable and strong motivations that had to be tapped into.

Loss of Identity

Time after time I saw people who were so beat down by their careers, they had lost their identity.

I started doing something at my meetings. Every time a new person arrived; I'd ask them to tell me something about themselves.

Let that phrase sink in. Tell me something about YOU.

Inevitably, people would respond with these replies:

> "I'm an engineer..."

> "I'm a secretary..."

> "I'm an accountant specializing in...."

It was always about the job. Seldom did anyone start with personal values like....

> "I'm a working mom who wants to find the right balance."

> "I'm passionate about helping people with their taxes."

This made me realize how so many people had absolutely lost their identities in their work.

I started boldly challenging people to get re-centered on who they were not what they did.

There's an old saying:

"Harness the power of your mind's attention and your heart's affection."

When you connect your intellect with your passion, you will become unstoppable.

I simply met too many people who had been operating with only half of that equation in play.

Life Lessons Ignored

There were other things to observe too.

People were openly sharing that the career path they had been on was never really their desire.

Leaving home, perhaps getting married early forced them into jobs just to get a paycheck.

One job led to another and soon a whole career emerged that was never aligned with the passion they had.

People knew they were dissatisfied but kept working the same old path to keep the income coming.

They never were bold enough to say 'I quit.'

I started telling people "Look, you're out of work. Why NOT look at the exact direction you want?"

I put several more observations to work and made a list.

STRIVE is Born

Then I scrambled the list to put them in a sequence of events that made sense.

I walked through the list with my colleagues.

Everyone agreed.

The initials of the first word or thought of every part spelled *STRIVE.*

Some of my buddies hated the word **strive**. They said it sounded like work.

"Job search is work." I said.

So, there it was. STRIVE became the model.

Since its inception in 2010, I've taught the STRIVE model to thousands of job seekers. I conducted workshops and webinars.

I've made a few changes to it, but for the most part, it exists today exactly as it first did back then.

In the remaining chapters I am going to introduce STRIVE. I'll be showing you the ways you too can apply the core principles to your search for the right job.

But before we begin, there are several things you need to consider.

CHAPTER 1 - BITTER OR BETTER?

Regardless of the circumstances that brought you to looking for a new job, there is a big question to ask yourself.

Right now, are you bitter or better for what has happened?

Here's the scenario: life throws you a curve ball. Things don't go your way. You suffer an embarrassing moment in front of colleagues, your spouse or your kids. You lose the deal, the game, the promotion, or the moment. The other guy wins. You failed. What are your responses?

Yes, I believe there is more than one. Of course, you'll have an immediate response. However, the sting of losing can linger near term, long term and for life. How do you react?

I've certainly lost out a few times. It's a natural part of a competitive commerce model. The chance to win or lose is all around us.

The key question is a very simple one... Do you become Bitter or Better?

Bitter

Do you get bitter over the issue? Will you allow anger or other negative emotions to rule the little place in that video library of your mind?

Every time the mention of that moment comes up, will you lash out, thinking or making very vile comments, turning red, and huffing off to simmer in the juices of self-pity all over again? Do you let relationships suffer over that moment?

Sometimes people make a vow to "never let that happen again".

Staying bitter over the issue has no real positive effects at all. In fact, being bitter has been proven to impact your health. Blood pressure, ulcers, and a host of other factors can build over time as we stew over the bad thoughts and bitterness caused by losing moments.

Those who study emotional intelligence will tell you the way you shift out of being bitter and the speed at which you do it is an indicator of your emotional intelligence scale.

Bitterness impacts your outward personality too. People can tell what you are thinking. Having a sour disposition will impair any ability to make and keep meaningful connections.

Better

Or are you the kind of person that will make it better? By better, I am talking about assessing the whole truth of the circumstance openly and objectively. Then finding a nugget of gold with which you may prosper by changing some area of your life and thinking:

- your technical/professional knowledge
- your behaviors
- your emotions

By making one or all these choices, the next time something similar arises, (and it will), you can respond in a much more positive way.

John Maxwell says "Experience is not good learning. Only informed learning from experience teaches us new things."

Being better also means forgiving any person or group who may have been the source of the bad moment. That little mental video I mentioned should not include the replay of the look on someone else's face when they "got you".

If you are focused on being better for the experience, you can more quickly advance and get un-stuck.

You won't be wallowing in the negative. Instead you will be inspiring to others. The sunshine will shine brightly.

When something bad happens, you have just two choices.

Will you be *Bitter or Better?*

Let it go. Be BETTER!

CHAPTER 2 - YOU ARE NOT YOUR JOB

If you lost your job today, what would that do to your sense of self-worth? Maybe you are reading this because you have lost your job.

Are you OK with it, or would you really suffer? Would you be worried about what your spouse, children, family and friends think about you because you lost the job?

In the beginning, the financial crisis of 2007-08 was mentioned. The organization Jobs Ministry Southwest was created. We started hosting a weekly gathering known as "The Main Event". Soon we had over 250 people attending our weekly workshops, hearing our speakers, and using our materials.

We had all the usual things you would expect from a job assistance organization (resume writing, interviewing skills coaching, networking, social media, etc.). For me though, what I quickly figured out was the phenomenon of how people dealt with job loss.

First, there was a huge common split between men and women. Men looked at their jobs for their significance. When I asked a man to tell me something about himself, 99% of the time he went straight to talking about his job. The story included job title, role, reach, budget, team size, and so forth. I had not asked what he <u>did</u> for a living. I asked to know something about them.

Women on the other hand, talked about a sense of security. The job gave them security. This usually translated into financial security, but often included the notion that at work they could be safe from whatever may be happening outside of work. Yes, this includes domestic violence, substance abuse, and other horrific things we see in the news.

You can only imagine how losing the job caused devastation in either direction. Men would often express losing their actual identities over a job loss. "I am not an engineer anymore; I am going to have to become a fry cook." (No disrespect to any type of position or work intended here). Women losing their jobs were emotionally wreaked for having lost their security; fear became the primary emotion.

Coaching hundreds of these folks individually, I found myself revisiting this common thread far too often. I spent a lot of time helping people re-center their core beliefs about who they were, what they were made of, and differentiating the job loss circumstance from their inner being.

It was no small task. When someone has interwoven these beliefs for decades, trying to untangle that mess was daunting. Sadly, not everyone made it through the mental shift. For those who did though, a whole new outlook drove them to seek new ideas, even new careers, to better align with what they discovered were their true values.

Separating the job from who you are is the key.

The Need

The need is to learn how to begin separating the job from the self. That's lousy grammar, but it gets to the point.

First let's talk about how we even get to that point in life. My wife and I are in the grandparent stage of our lives. Our kids are grown and married, having their own children. We have four grandkids and counting.

As we celebrate the birth and bringing the new babies home, I have observed a few key thoughts. None of those babies left the hospital with a smart phone, a business card, a laptop or an iPad. They weren't waiting on the next call or rushing to the next appointment or shift change. Their only 'job' was to eat, sleep, and, well you know what.

When did the identity thing start shifting away from what it was at birth to what it becomes for so many Americans? Where does this sense of work and vocation creep in and drive the definition of personal significance?

I like to refer to the story of the frog in the pot. The story goes that you put a frog in cool water, in a pot on the stove. Then start turning up the heat slowly. Eventually the water boils and the frog dies. If you boil the water first, then drop the frog in, he jumps right out.

So many situations in life are this way. We get into a scenario. Over time, the circumstances change, pressures bold, attitudes shift, and eventually we are at a whole new place.

Believe me I know about competitive forces at work - the push to win the next promotion, get the right recognition, and get that next raise. All of it becomes a focus for anyone hoping to prosper in the workplace. As these things accumulate, our culture tends to honor the achievements.

We stand in awe of our corporate giants, people who have climbed the ladder as we say. It is easy to feel proud of those accomplishments.

For each new rung on the ladder though, a bit of our identity gets painted with a new brush. We start becoming the job.

Again though, the need here is to distance our definition of self from the job description we have.

Satisfaction of the Need

So how do we ever start making this happen? How can we separate our identity from the jobs we hold so dear?

What might be some of the hurdles to overcome? Well, here are the ones I have seen over the years in my business.

Poor self-esteem - This one might have been overdone in years past. Yet it remains as a key driver. Why? When our individual understanding and belief about our sense of self has been damaged, we naturally look for a substitute.

We look for something to latch on to that can fill that void deep inside us. It's a kind of replacement thinking. The job is a huge part of our life, so why not let our new statement of what we are be about the job.

Well, the logic might not be bad, but the result is dangerous. Why? Because if the job opportunity evaporates as it did for so many in 2008, what do you have?

You get pushed right back into that sense of failure, inadequacy, and so forth.

This sounds too ethereal - "Everything you're talking about Doug sounds bogus." Really? All I can tell you is that I have firsthand experience with thousands of job seekers who needed to get this right before they could land their next gig.

When the economy is throwing lemons, a person needs a really centered belief system to avoid getting down on themselves about the situation. It can happen to anyone.

Bad tapes playing in your mind - Losing a job has a lot of unhealthy consequences. The biggest one is the risk that those old tapes in your brain start playing. You know what I am talking about.

The tape with the teacher telling you how bad you are. The one with the sibling riding you about something you did feel bad about but didn't need to be reminded of. And worst of all is the look in the mirror where you see a very poor image looking back.

I know these bad tape topics can go on and on.

None of these are good for you. And frankly, I have yet to find a case study where the truth was anything close to being as bad as what the person claimed as their downside.

Visualization

By understanding this overall dynamic and the relationship between job and self, you can free yourself of the disappointment, guilt, fear, and uncertainty when your job is adversely impacted or lost.

When the job situation changes enough you no longer have to trigger all of those emotions.

By redefining your purpose and sense of self, you can more quickly focus your energy when the job situation changes.

The rollercoaster effect does not have to have such severe highs and lows. Oh, job change is never easy, but by disconnecting your value system from the significance of the work, you reach a better, more realistic view of what the job should be and where it fits in the scheme of things.

Action

So how do you get there? Here are a few action items to consider.

Test yourself in advance.

Ask the key question - will I be OK if I were to lose my job? I mean really dive deep on that one. If the answer is "NO, I won't be OK, emotionally I'll be ruined", then you might be dealing with this troubling idea that your self-worth is too closely bound to your job.

I will grant you the obvious issues that arise from such a question. I am saying to set aside the financial impact. Focus on the psychological and emotional things that are spun up when you entertain this question, things like fear, doubt, anger, hostility.

Experts tell us these kinds of emotions are symptomatic of deeper root causes. I contend that having your job tied to your identity is a pretty big root.

Ask others

Ask your closest friend and confidants. Ask these folks what they think about your balance for work versus sense of self. Hint: a spouse is not always the best person to ask this question. This is true simply because they have too much vested and at stake.

Imagine going a whole new direction with work

If your opportunity to make money went a whole new way, would losing the former position or job impact your definition of yourself.

This can help determine how proud you are of the current situation. Pride is usually indicative of tying it to some sense of self-worth. If something is boosting some area of your mental image, you are often proud of it.

Try to define who and what you are without mentioning work

Try this one day. See if you like the statement you have. If not, take some time to work on that.

Let me say this theme has been played out in many lives I know. It seems to be human nature to let our work become a definition of what we are.

I encourage you to do yourself a favor. If your identity and sense of self-worth is tied too closely to your job, start the process I've presented here. Work through the issues and create a new story for yourself.

Disclaimer – The materials and information presented here are not a substitute for professional psychological counseling. If your situation needs further help, seek the services of a licensed professional counselor.

THE MODEL

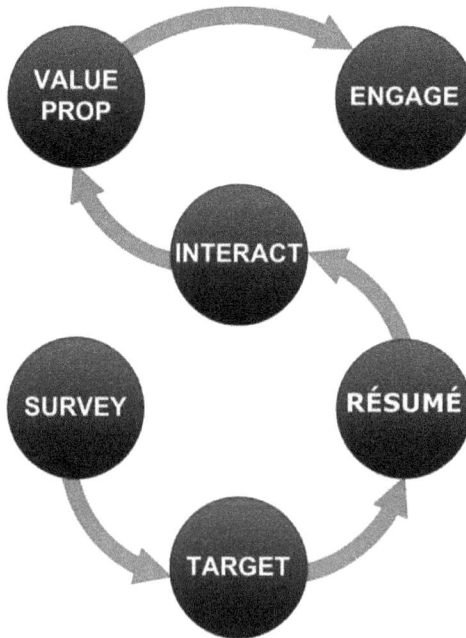

STEP 1 – SURVEY

Survey is the first step in the STRIVE Model. Survey is really about your effort to regain your identity.

I like the word *survey* because it conjures up the idea of looking around, looking back, looking forward, and side-to-side. Taking an inventory.

Specifically, for job search it means taking an inventory of your experiences.

Here is where you begin building a list of accomplishments which you will use later in the resume writing and interviewing process.

More importantly though, for now, you need to attach significance to the list you write.

We've all had accomplishments in our careers that were great and significant.

But we've also done things that might have been good for the business or the company where you worked but you left saying "I never want to do that again."

This is the kind of significance I'm talking about.

Look at the things you put on your list, your written list.

I stress getting this list written down because you will need it later.

It's not good enough to just spend some time meditating on a list without writing it down.

WRITE IT DOWN

Plus, by writing it down you can focus on the various items and begin to see a pattern emerging.

Pretty soon you will be able to highlight the great accomplishments you loved doing versus those that you did not.

Pay attention to the sense of connection you get from this list.

If you're fortunate to have had positive experiences along the way, GREAT! Celebrate that. Let those become your professional persona.

BUT....

If you don't feel good about the collective impact of this list, you just may have been spending your time in the wrong area or the wrong job.

Work on this list for a while. Don't just knock it out over a weekend. Let it simmer and marinate in your mind.

PERSONAL VISION STATEMENT

In this survey step, you may also want to perform a Personal Vision analysis on yourself.

If you're a person who just lets life happen without any intentionality to it, now might be the BEST time to do a Personal Vision Quest for the first time

If you've done something like this before and you need to change jobs, be very sure you refresh your personal vision before you do anything else.

What is Personal Vision?

According to a dear friend and colleague, Dr. John Younker, PhD, the Personal Vision Statement is as follows.

Definition: *A vision statement describes the "ideal future state" of an individual and/or an organization.* It energizes and mobilizes the individual(s) to realize this ideal. It empowers people and creates enthusiasm describing the unique and distinctive contributions that the individual(s) will make in the chosen field of endeavor.

The Vision is a statement that communicates: *"This is what makes me/us special/unique and what we foresee as our ideal future state."*

Discussion: The Individual (Personal) Vision Statement is an individual person's formal declaration of intent that describes his/her ideal future state. In the case of an organizational situation (i.e. company, relationship/family, work team), the organizational vision statement is also a formal declaration of intent.

Additionally, the organizational vision statement is the result of the effective integration of the individual members' needs ... the key stakeholders ... with the needs of the overall organization.

For individuals, It is a rather personal statement, which must be responsive to some level of diversity in views/perceptions, changing trends, ever evolving challenges and opportunities and environmental (physical, financial, spiritual conditions. The organizational vision statement vividly describes the *"kind of organization we want to become" and "how we want to be perceived."*

The Personal Vision Statement lends itself to being summarized or condensed into a series of short descriptive phrases, images, slogans and other devices that invite people to embrace it and own it.

It provides substance with which an individual or individuals can identify and associate with pride. The Vision Statement captures people's attention with its zest and boldness ... *To go where no man has gone before*.

The statement may be the precursor of the Mission Statement (statement of purpose). In situations where a well-defined and currently viable mission already exists, the Vision may articulate how an individual or organization will improve upon its performance.

For the STRIVE Model, the discipline of building a Personal Vision Statement helps to:

> **"begin with the end in mind."**
> **~Stephen R. Covey**

By defining your future state, you can better design your job search to properly fit the needs of that future state rather than the other way around i.e. arriving one day at some destination, not knowing where or what that might be.

There is much more on creating your own Personal Purpose Vision in the Bonus section at the end of this book.

STEP 2 – TARGET

Target is the next step in the STRIVE Model. Targeting is about deciding on the type of company has the right job opportunities that fit your survey results.

Remember, this whole process is about better aligning your future vision of yourself with the career path that makes sense.

Too many before you have taken jobs hoping to build a lifestyle only to find they have spent years, perhaps decades in pursuit of a job history that becomes very unfulfilling.

DON'T MAKE THAT MISTAKE AGAIN

The results of your Survey step should help define a purpose and a detailed vision of what you should be striving to achieve through your job.

Why would you consider applying with a company that either doesn't do what you want to do or provide the kind of jobs that do those things?

I realize the bigger the company, the harder it may become to identify the right opportunities, but that leads to the next part of the targeting step.

You must do the research to find these jobs.

Whether thru job postings (which for the record are my least favorite job sources) or doing your own research, finding and targeting the right companies is your best alternative for creating this perfect career alignment.

If your survey step leads you to the vision of becoming a world class purple squirrel hunter, then start looking up everything you can find about purple squirrels.

Where do they live? What do the eat? When do they wake up? You must figure these things out.

These clues lead you to sources where there are better fits for your vision.

OK, purple squirrel hunter too much?

How about graphic designer?

OK, what kind of graphics? Fashion? Business? Education?

Start with these big picture ideas and begin distilling it.

What kind of graphic designer? Business. OK great, what part about business?

Technical manuals? Marketing?

Marketing. Ok, perfect. Now which media? Web based, print, art?

Keep chiseling away at the definition of the things that fit your vision. Soon you will find references to companies who do those things and have jobs doing those things.

Once you start identifying the companies that HAVE the jobs, you can create another list to itemize those companies.

Whether you are focused on a single company or list of companies, the next part of targeting is to identify potential contacts within those companies.

Hands down, LinkedIn has become the premier source for finding this valuable intelligence in the market.

If you are not yet a user of LinkedIn, you are truly missing out. There are numerous training modules provided by LinkedIn for free to help you understand the many ways you can explorer the database and make contacts. (More on LinkedIn at the end).

STEP 3 – RESUME

Resume is the third step in the STRIVE Model. Yes, we're finally going to talk about resumes.

It's still odd to me that when I hear about someone changing jobs the first thing, they think of is "better update my resume."

Update it for what? Just so you can have a stale list of old news. NO!!!

You cannot write a meaningful resume without a purpose. Resumes should never be just about your job history. They should be a story about the future.

How can that be?

Let me show you.

We've just gone through steps 1 and 2. You surveyed your history and decided on a future vision.

Next you targeted companies that fit that vision. Here is where you connect with a story that excites that potential employer to pick YOU!

Your resume should be *the story* that helps a prospective employer understand how you are going to make them money or save them money.

33

There are really no other choices. Even with highly skilled and specialized roles like doctors, they too must land positions.

The prestigious positions ultimately translate into someone somewhere making or saving money.

There is no other game.

Some will argue with me on this point. That's OK. If you try to tell me something about your vision being saving starving children halfway around the world, I'd say wonderful! But is that a career path or a mission? Big difference.

For the sake of this writing, we are talking about paying jobs with entities that exist for delivering goods or services.

BACK TO THE POINT

Your resume needs to be that story. "Your company needs X. I do X. I do it very well. I've been doing it. Here are some examples where I helped someone else make or save money doing X."

That's the bulk of the story.

In the Introduction I mentioned cutting back on long form two-page resumes. Why?

Because the resume is just a tool to get you in the door. Nothing more.

If a screener is put off by the page count in your resume and throws it in the trash without ever reading it, there is no value in all that detail.

Instead, you need to think like a marketer.

You need to WOW the reader with content "above the fold."

Did you know that's how newspapers and magazines sell their most volume? They put juicy, eye-catching information above the fold of the paper.

In the case of magazines, it's on the cover.

How does that apply to resumes? Take a standard letter sized piece of paper. Fold it in half, top to bottom. Now you have the fold.

In one half a sheet, the top half, you need to grab the reader's attention.

Hint #1 – Employers don't care about YOUR statement of purpose here.

Example: I am seeking a challenging position hunting large North American purple squirrels.

Who cares what you want? Sorry, no one does just yet. They will eventually, but not now. More on that later.

Rather, you need to say "Your company needs X. I do X. I do it very well. I've been doing it. Here are some examples where I helped someone else make or save money doing X."

Then support that claim by inserting matching accomplishments from your accomplishments inventory. (Step 1 Survey material). I told you we'd use those again.

Selectively choose 3 to 5 items that fit the one company your targeting right now.

You're writing a custom-tailored resume, one company at a time.

By the way, a well-written accomplishment cites what you did and what it resulted in.

"I designed a process for squirrel trapping that increased catches per trap by 50%."

"I managed a team of squirrel hunters that caught 15% more squirrels year over year."

The metrics you can quantify in these accomplishment statements help the prospective employer translate immediate worth in their own company.

When they see examples like this, they are doing the math in their head.

"Wow, 50% more catches per trap. In my company that means $50,000."

Now they are interested in meeting you and hearing more about who you are.

SALES MINDED APPROACH

Everything from this point forward must be sales minded.

I know that turns many people off. But you ARE selling; selling yourself, your skills, and your abilities.

You are selling to intentionally get on track with your vision.

Now, that said, you can do hard sell or soft sell. You choose based on your personality. Yet somehow you will be selling.

THE JOB HISTORY

Let's get your job history out of the way.

Based on all my experience helping thousands of job seekers, I have a few pet peeves about the way people try to list job history.

The first, and my all-time biggest objection is your job titles.

Listing your experience using the funky job titles your old employer gave you creates far more trouble than its worth.

Here's how job titles work.

I was once managing a large department at a big regional bank. We had thousands of employees. I needed a new position in my group.

I submitted a rough draft of a job description to HR. They did their analysis. Then they asked me what I wanted to call it. I didn't care. I just needed a qualified candidate to fill the seat.

The next thing you know, I had a new position with a strange job title. The job title sort of described what we were doing, but never came close to describing the real value I needed from that person.

Once this person left, I'm guessing they took that job title with them while they were applying for their next job.

Heaven help them if it helped get them another job.

What do you do on your resume?

I suggest and coach the idea of writing your own job titles. Make them be consistent with the work you did.

More importantly they need to be consistent with the job you want and the job the potential company you want to target already has.

I can already hear the scoffers calling me crazy.

Follow this thought. Name the old position whatever you want. If the new employer checks on anything, it is doubtful the former employer will even get down to that detail.

Usually when the reference calls happen, old employers are trained to divulge only a confirmation that you worked there plus a to and from date. Nothing more gets shared.

The old employer will not spill the beans.

Even if they do (and I promise you most won't), you can explain to your new employer you were trying to be clear about the discussion. You never felt the old job title fit the role very well.

After all, you did disclose the times you were at the old company, right? You weren't trying to withhold anything.

Besides, if you get this far into the opportunity, this will not be a problem.

STEP 4 – INTERACT

Interact is the fourth step in the STRIVE Model. I bet you were thinking "I" was for interviews. Not yet.

To get to the interview stage, there must be interaction of several kinds. I'll list these in no particular order.

First, you should be reaching out to everyone in the various circles you may be in, family, community, ex-associates, and new names.

Yes, you need to work to build new relationships too.

But let's talk about the people you know first. Be sure that your closest contacts know where you are in your search. Help them help you.

What does that mean?

I've heard it said the next-door neighbor's five-year-old daughter ought to be able to explain what you do for work. Create a simple to understand statement of what you do and what you might be looking for.

By doing this, others can help you. If they hear people talking at the coffee shop, they can connect the dots.

On the other hand, if your story is too complicated, people worry about getting it mixed up or they just don't understand, so they feel helpless to help.

Change that. Get the word out.

NETWORKING ELSEWHERE

Now let's turn to the topic of networking. I truly believe that networking for job seekers is a no-man's land. I've watched people spend a great amount of time and money attending useless gatherings under the guise of doing something meaningful toward their job search.

Too often these meetings are filled with attendees who have no job. They can't help someone else find a job because they themselves are out of work.

Yes, they might have some contacts to share, but most often the time goes by with little to show for it.

There is one key exception to this otherwise disappointing behavior. Trade shows and conventions are far more fertile ground.

At least by going to a trade show, you stand a better than average chance of meeting people from the exact companies you targeted.

WHAT YOU SAY

People often ask me "What should I really say or do at a networking event?"

The thing you don't start with is "Hi, I was wondering if you can help me find a job."

No, instead you need to focus on making the connection with people. Politely introduce yourself. Quickly turn the discussion to the other person.

It's a well-documented fact that people feel the best connected with a stranger when the stranger has done less of the talking. Be prepared to ask good questions about the other person.

What is your position?

How long have you been with that company?

Have you had the opportunity to move around a lot?

Inevitably, when you can guide the discussion to be more about the other person, they will walk away thinking "Wow, they were interesting. I wouldn't mind talking with them again."

Leave people with that feeling, then you can follow up with a message about how great it was to meet them. Thank them for the conversation.

Then you can slip in the tease about your job search.

"Oh, by the way, I've been looking at opportunities at your company. I specifically can do X. Would you mind referring me to someone there who I might talk to?"

STEP 5 – VALUE PROP

Value Proposition is the fifth and a critical step in the STRIVE Model.

Having a personal value proposition is what gets you past the resume and through the interview. Value proposition is another way to tell your brand story.

You are a brand. If you've never thought of yourself that way, now is the time to start.

Just as in the resume step, you need to be thinking about presenting yourself as a story; selling what you can deliver.

Now though, your story needs to be deeper than the resume. You must be able to articulate YOUR value to the interviewer or the hiring manager.

Every possible answer to every question should lead you back to this core value proposition.

Become convinced you are the answer to the company's need in the position they are asking you about.

Building your value proposition can be easier if you did a good job during your survey step building the accomplishments list.

That list of great accomplishments gives you all the fuel you will ever need to establish a good value proposition.

People have told me fascinating stories about taking their accomplishments inventory list to the interview.

Then when the interviewer says "Tell me about a time when you....." the candidate turns to their list. Pausing a bit they respond "Well, once I was responsible for this and that..."

There have been times where the interviewer asks, "What are you reading from?" The candidate replies "Oh this is my complete accomplishments list. Here, let me give you a copy."

Every time I have heard that story, the candidate has won the job.

YOU see, by having great answers to back-up your value proposition you lock in that value to the prospective employer. Add in a touch of being very well prepared for the interview by having this amazing list, and BANG! The job will be yours.

CONFIDENCE

There's another subtle benefit of doing all this preparation.

YOU WILL FEEL MORE CONFIDENT!

Guaranteed.

The person with the best preparation usually has the best confidence in the situation.

If you know your history by being able to reflect on written accomplishments, you can be much more confident in your presentation of your value proposition.

Couple this with good preparation from having targeted the company (step 2). You will be unstoppable.

STEP 6 – ENGAGE

Engage is the sixth and final step.

You shouldn't do all the work to win the job without having a plan for making it stick.

That is where engage comes to play.

"We're at our best when we feel connected to each other." – Bruce Daisley

Being engaged in the new job has to do with learning the ropes, meeting the people, building relationship, and finding ways to do the things you presented in your resume and value proposition.

Let's break this down.

Doing what you do.
If you were successful at defining key roles and values, the ones that won you the job, why would you ignore them once you start work?

You wouldn't, right?

Now is the time to show off. Not in a bad way, but in a positive way, demonstrating the very thing(s) that won you the job.

Whatever your special skill, now is the time to dive in with your on-boarding, asking great questions, and setting YOURSELF up for success nor failure.

Learn the tools and procedures they give you. Don't be shy to ask solid questions about the work.

However, PLEASE, don't make yourself a turn-off by belittling the things you learn. If your experience has a better way to do something, pace yourself and pick the right time to share that information. Don't be the person jumping up saying "Well, where I came from we did this SOOOO much better."

You want to be building connections right now, not turning people off.

Learn the Team

Get to know the people on your team. Don't go overboard here either but let yourself be personable. Politely answer questions about yourself. Share the right information without being overbearing or smug.

Be relatable.

The old schoolyard saying is "If you want a friend, be a friend."

That is so true. If you want to build a network at work, you must be available to network yourself. There is no harm in being the first to reach across for connection.

More importantly, get to know who knows what on your team. Every team known to man has had a mix of talents and skills. Otherwise we'd all be clones.

Learn what others know so you can connect and leverage those skills.

No one likes anything more in a work environment than being able to talk about their work, not yours, but theirs.

Politely get engaged asking about that.

Do the Little Things

Unless you're the CEO, no job on the floor or in the area is beneath you.

When my kids got their first big jobs after college, I encouraged them to be a great team player.

How do you do that?

Well, if the copier is out of paper, learn how to refill it. Don't ask someone else to do it for you.

If someone left a mess in the break room, help clean it up.

Do the little bit extra to show people you are on the team. Yes, you might argue "I'm the only one doing those things." So what? What's the harm?

You will get out of a situation what you put into the situation.

Besides, if you get a reputation as being the person who helps get all those things done, who do you think would be the LAST person a boss would want to get rid of should things get tight on budget?

Not you, my friend.

Be Real

'Fake it 'til you make it' only goes so far. You will get found out. Figure out what being real looks like on you. Don't be overly extroverted if you're an introvert. And vice versa.

You should have a good idea of who you are and what you're about because of the earlier steps in this model.

Let those attributes shine.

Nothing is more natural than being naturally YOU.

Stay true to yourself.

Conclusion - A CAUTIONARY TALE

Back to the Jobs Ministry story. We coached over 4,500 job seekers during our time providing career transition services. The data showed us 66% of the clients using the services found jobs.

That percentage didn't make me happy. I wanted to know more about the 33% that didn't land jobs.

As the data was studied, something very interesting emerged.

The client population was segmented into **three very distinct groups**. The headcount in each group resulted in an exact third, third and third distribution. So, 33%, 33% and 33% respectively.

The first group was the **Over-Achievers.** This group jumped in, absorbed the material, took the training, and got busy doing every step in the model.

They didn't argue. They didn't create other alternatives. They consumed what we were teaching.

Most importantly, they didn't stay stuck where they were. They got busy. Old mindsets about former employers were quickly forgotten.

Nothing but new direction was in their vision.

The next group was the **So-So Performers.** This group paid attention, but occasionally questioned the newness of the ideas. They pushed back a little.

Yet, in the end, they too went to work. They figured out what they needed to do with the model and got it done.

These two group together made up the 66% success mark. Or said another way, we saw 100% success in each of the first two groups.

Sadly, we saw 100% fail in the last group. WHY?

When we started looking closely at the final third, we realized these folks were the ones who were stuck with psychological and emotional scars.

The hatred and bitterness for their former companies was severe. The mindset about looking forward was blinded by old hurts and wounds.

Attitude was insurmountable.

These folks balked at every point in the STRIVE model. They made up unflattering names for the steps we taught.

They argued with presenters who were trying to help. They all had the little dark cloud above their head, making them hard to talk to and difficult to reason with.

In the end, they sulked home to do nothing. Frankly, I never heard from many of them again. If they eventually found work, I never heard about it. No doubt it was not because of something we tried to teach them.

REFLECTION

Upon my own reflection, I realized this metric was true in every organization. The workforce follows this same 3-way distribution.

The top tier is the rock stars. They do most of the work. The second tier are reliable but won't necessarily take on more work voluntarily. They do good work, but if you're the manager you must direct every step.

The last tier ends up being the ones who cause the most trouble. They often stay on disciplinary warning. If reductions in workforce are required, they are the first ones on the list to go.

Now, all that said, if you grabbed this book and are reading it right now, I seriously doubt you are anywhere close to being in this last third of the population. If by chance you are one of those folks, may God be with you. Nothing will work until you change your attitude.

Now, back to everyone else.

You, likely, are looking for better ways to get ahead. Good for you!

You've bene given the STRIVE model. Study each step and get busy. As another help, I've added several Bonus sections for you to enjoy.

BONUS 1 – PERSONAL PURPOSE AND VISION

"Without Vision, the people perish." ~ Proverbs

In Step 1 of STRIVE, you are asked to do a "survey". That is basically the same as deciding on a Personal Purpose Vision Statement. Here is a proven process to build and define your personal purpose.

"Vison without action is merely a dream. Action without vision just passes the time. Vision with action can change the world."

~Joel Barker

The following text is contributed by Monte Pendleton (Pendleton, 2013), *co-founder and Past President of Silver Fox Advisors, Houston, Texas.*

Being On Purpose promises you amazing freedom, power and pleasure. And the truth is, it's not difficult. Our true Purpose in life is merely to express who we already are right now.

As we begin fully doing this, we benefit both ourselves and others by becoming A ROLE MODEL of who we truly already are in such a way that it provides an example to all of those in our lives; inspiring them and thereby making a significant difference in our world.

Our Personal Purpose will unfold quickly and easily as we investigate the philosophical conversation concerning 'Be/Do/Have' that is said to have begun over 5,000 years ago.

Even though it has held the interest of 'human potential' scholars for that long, it is only now beginning to play a role in the important task of unfolding our own Personal Purpose.

Man's normal approach to life is reversed into 'Do/Have/Be.' It begins with doing instead of being, e.g., do your homework, then you'll have an education, and then you'll be a doctor.

This approach misleads us into thinking that it is what we do that makes the most difference. It causes us to spend much of our life 'doing' in order to get ready to 'have' our results and then 'be' somebody. For instance, study hard, to get educated, and be magnificent.

The truth is, the real difference we make in life is made, not by what we do, but by expressing who we already are (be). We already are magnificent.

We are a unique combination of virtues and qualities that have prepared us for a special task in life, to be on purpose in our world.

Certainly, the qualities that we 'BE' must be expressed in our activities, our 'doing,' or we couldn't be a role model. Therefore, to be on purpose we must first identify those special qualities and then find a job or activity at which we can best express or demonstrate them.

If we can truly 'get it,' at a profound level, that we are endowed by our Maker with unlimited power and ability, we will accept the grand Purpose God has for us and we will create grand results.

We'll contribute far more by expressing our true, natural, ever-present magnificence, than we ever could by trying to improve on ourselves, trying to become someone we are not.

The truth is, who we are makes a far more significant difference than what we do. For instance, being a role model of honesty and integrity for our children will be of far greater value than years of working to feed them.

We undoubtedly need to do both, but our living examples of love, integrity and spirituality will ultimately be remembered as the greater service.

So, for any of us to maximize our personal effectiveness and contribution in life, we must know at a profound level

1) who we are,

2) what we have been called on to exemplify, and

3) to whom we will model it.

We will do some exercises on the following pages that will enable us to self-discover the answers to these three questions.

Why are these answers important? Because when we know and role model our virtues and qualities to the world, we are naturally attractive. We attract the friends, the opportunities, the happiness we are meant to have.

Life will flow with fun, excitement and success. Our efforts will truly bless all involved; our family, friends, fellow workers, associates, customers and employers. We best serve when we best role model who we are and what we stand for.

Also, we can accomplish far more in life when we employ a team effort. If we intend to succeed in a big way, we need to know precisely who we are and what is on Purpose for us, and then we can communicate and role model that information to the team we enlist to assist us.

Only to the degree that we communicate our Purpose, Vision and Goals to our friends, family, mentors and associates, can they know how to effectively support and assist us in having all God intended us to have. Any support, coaching or advice given to us without considering what is 'on Purpose' for us will automatically be, to some degree, off Purpose.

When we are fully communicating to our entire team, we will probably experience, for the first time, the thrill of having everyone "pulling on the same end of the rope." Our projects will soar.

The answers required to generate our Purpose are not difficult. We already know them at a deep level. Our problem is that they are difficult to recognize and communicate to others because we have our be's, do's and have's all mixed up together in our thinking.

We must sort them out and organize them before we can truly put them to work for us. Filling in the statements on the following pages will enable you to separate your Purpose (who you be), from your Vision (dreams, haves) and from your Goals (actions, do's).

Dr. John DeMartini discovered that each of us loves to be "on Purpose" in life. Therefore, you can best discover your Purpose by sorting out what you would love to "be, do and have". By writing down your "loves" in this process, you can quickly unscramble your thinking.

In Step 1 you will weigh the eight key life areas and prioritize them in order of importance to you. Then, in Step 2, you will list the qualities you'd love to be expressing. These (be's) will be included as part of your Personal Purpose statement. Next, in Step 3, you will create your Personal Visions (have's), and then in Step 4, choose your Goals, (do's) the action steps to support your Vision. These four steps are then combined to comprise your Personal Purpose Statement.

Being On Purpose opens a whole new paradigm for you, one of possibilities instead of problems. Better still, you are able to use it to enroll others into making your dreams come true. However, to get your Purpose statement done, there is a price you must pay.

You must over-ride your ego, that little voice in your head that is right now telling you that being on Purpose will be a pain and will take all the fun out of life, it will be too much work. Don't believe it.

You will love being on purpose because it gives you permission to be exactly who you'd love to be, do what you would love to do, and have what you would love to have.

Step 1: Ranking Your Eight Key Life Facets

Key Life Facet Definitions:

Career: Refers to what you do for a living, your job, vocation, profession, occupation, position, or business.

Family: Refers to the quality of relationship, activities, quality time, harmony and closeness of your family.

Financial: Refers to your income, net worth, investments, security, budget, retirement savings and lifestyle.

Mental: Refers to your expansion and growth in knowledge wisdom, skills, experience, attitude and peace of mind.

Physical: Refers to your health, physical fitness, capability, endurance, strength, weight, appearance and wellbeing.

Relationships: Refers to your friendships, social network, co-workers, colleagues, companions, outside of family.

Spiritual: Refers to your faith, source of inspiration, conscience, understanding, relationship, guidance and trust.

Serving: Refers to your need to volunteer, serve others, to contribute to society, give back and make a difference.

To begin with, carefully consider the above eight key life definitions. Awareness of, and participation in all eight is necessary for a well-rounded life. You will now rank them in the order of importance to YOU at this time.

Ranking these Life Facets will help you discover your personal priorities and better understand what motivates you. This exercise is invaluable because it enables you to know and communicate to others how and why you are prioritizing your time and resources, and what is motivating you.

Now, prioritize these in the order of importance that each one holds for you. There are no right or wrong answers, and everyone's answers will be different because our priorities are different. The key areas are arranged below in pairs to aid you in evaluating them.

Begin by circling the one item in each pair that is your first choice or highest priority. Continue until you have circled one item from each pair.

8. Serving

5. Physical

1. Career

4. Mental

7. Spiritual

4. Mental

2. Family

8. Serving

1. Career

5. Physical

6. Relationships

7. Spiritual

8. Serving

4. Mental

4. Mental

3. Financial

3. Financial

5. Physical

5. Physical

4. Mental

6. Relationship

1. Career

5. Physical

6. Relationship

2. Family

1. Career

8. Serving

6. Relationship

6. Relationship

2. Family

3. Financial

6. Relationship

6. Relationship

4. Mental

7. Spiritual

1. Career

7. Spiritual

8. Serving

3. Financial

2. Family

5. Physical

7. Spiritual

3. Financial

1. Career

2. Family

7. Spiritual

1. Career

8. Serving

2. Family

4. Mental

2. Family

5. Physical

3. Financial

7. Spiritual

3. Financial

8. Serving

Now count the number of times on the previous page that you have circled each life area and enter that number below.

Career   ____

Family   ____

Financial   ____

Mental   ____

Physical   ____

Relationships   ____

Spiritual   ____

Serving   ____

When finished, your total above should be 28.

Next you can chart the results.

Now, in the column below titled '1st Ranking,' place a number 1 beside the Key Area that had the largest total above. Place a 2 in the 1st Ranking column beside the Area that had the second largest total. Continue until all eight have been entered. If you have a tie, try to rank the most important one higher than the other.

AREA	1st Ranking	2nd Ranking	3rd Ranking	4th Ranking	5th Ranking	6th Ranking
Career						
Family						
Financial						
Mental						
Physical						
Relationships						
Spiritual						
Serving						

Look over your 1st Ranking very carefully. Ask yourself if it truly reflects your priorities in life. If not, try this simple exercise. Look at the Areas you have ranked 1 and 2.

If you could have only one of the two, which one would you choose? For example, if you had ranked Career and Family as 1 and 2, and if you had to choose between them, which one would you, choose? If there is a change, re-rank that Area as #1, placing your new ranking under the '2nd Ranking' column.

Then continue this exercise for the Areas now ranked 2 and 3, then Areas ranked 3 and 4, etc. As you continue your self-discovery your priorities may change, but it is important to know what they are presently.

Many ask why we need to work with all 8 Key Areas when they are only interested in two or three. The answer is that true happiness comes from a well-rounded life, one that addresses all 8 areas.

It is quite easy to address them all at the same time if we think about them and plan for them. If we don't, we usually focus on one or two, almost excluding the others, often causing disaster.

You may focus on your work or finances, only to end up neglecting family, health, spirituality, etc. People frequently end up with a fortune, only to discover they are involved in a divorce, heart attack, dependency or a dysfunctional family. This well-rounded approach will help you avoid those unfortunate and unhappy results in your life.

Look over the completed 2nd Ranking column. Repeat the exercise once more if you feel your second ranking is not yet correct, writing the results in the "3rd Ranking" column. When you feel your rankings are correct, go on to Step 2, "Unfolding Your Personal Purpose."

STRIVE for Job Search Success

Step 2: Unfolding Your Personal Purpose

Unfolding your Personal Purpose is another valuable source of self-discovery. Your Purpose is not something you choose; you already have it. You were born with it.

When you reveal your Purpose, it will probably surprise you by its profound magnificence. You have a BIG purpose and it is to Role Model your unique combination of qualities.

Remember, your Purpose is about who you will 'be', not what you do. When you be the person 'who you love to be most', that is being the most on Purpose.

Then, you will automatically do the right thing.

Begin now by writing four or five or more *Qualities* you would love to be expressing in each key area below. Use a single word for each quality. (e.g., integrity, health, love, joy, wisdom, kindness, etc.) Really go for it.

Look inside yourself, into your heart and include the most awesome and magnificent qualities that come to you. Don't leave any life area blank, and remember, there are no "right" or "wrong" answers.

If it is a quality you would love to be expressing, that is the right answer for you.

1)   In my Career, I would love to BE expressing

_____

_____

2)   With my Family, I would love to BE expressing

_____

_____

3)   Financially, I would love to BE expressing

_____

_____

4)   Mentally, I would love to BE expressing

_____

_____

5)   Physically, I would love to BE expressing

_____

_____

6)   In my Relationships, I would love to BE expressing

_____

_____

7)   Spiritually, I would love to BE expressing

_____

_____

8)   In Serving others, I would love to BE expressing

_____

_____

Having finished all of the eight prior statements, follow these instructions carefully:

Look at the qualities you listed and write the one most powerful and magnificent quality from each of the above eight key statements into the following space, eight total. Be bold, grand and far out.

In my life, I would love to BE expressing

_____
_____
_____
_____

Now, consider the ways that your 'role modeling' the above qualities will impact and serve all those that your life touches. Enter those ways below.

Expressing the **qualities** I love will impact those in my life by

_____

_____

_____

_____

_____

(e.g. teaching, inspiring, empowering, motivating, enabling, encouraging, etc.)

Next, think of the **individuals or groups** you would love to impact, and identify them below.

I would love to BE impacting my:

_____

_____

_____

(e.g. family, friends, workers, children, students, associates, etc.)

Now, review the example Personal Purpose Statement below.

EXAMPLE: "My Personal Purpose is to be a role model of enlightenment, wisdom, contribution, prosperity, love, intimacy, health, gratitude, happiness, satisfaction, and fun, which will inspire and empower my family, friends, clients, employees and associates."

Naturally your individual **Personal Purpose** will be quite different, but you can see how your Purpose Statement might look when your qualities, your impact, and your audiences are combined.

So, combine the above 3 parts of your Purpose statement until it is formatted similarly to the prior example. Then, polish it until it perfectly states who you are, and how and who you will serve.

Continue to revise your Personal Purpose Statement until you are satisfied with it. You may revise this statement many times before your Purpose is satisfactorily revealed.

My Personal Purpose is to be a role model of

_____

_____

_____

_____

which will

_____

_____

_____

my

_____

_____

_____

Being on Purpose will enable you "to make a significant difference in the world."

You are here to serve, empower, enable and encourage the people in your life in your own very special way. Don't resist it, don't let it frighten you.

It is only natural to be a little uncomfortable with it at first, but the sooner you align your life with it, the sooner you take responsibility for it, then, the sooner you will begin expressing maximum power, attraction and magnificent results.

You don't have to fear it because it will not be difficult. You will love being on Purpose. Remember, 'being on purpose' is merely being your true Self, role modeling the qualities you already 'love to be,' expressing to the world.

By now you may have noticed that you are already being pretty much the person you would love to be. You don't have to change much to "become" that person before you can get on Purpose and start producing the magnificent results you were created to produce.

You may ask, "don't I need to do something different?" The answer is "probably very little". If you are willing to role model who you really love to be, you will be **on Purpose…..your Purpose.**

However, you may choose to quit doing some things. If you are 'running a number' or 'putting on an act' like cavalier, tough, helpless, worldly, clown, dumb, limited, abused, unloved, or victim, you may choose to stop doing that after you see how much it is costing you.

Role modeling these old 'vices' is unattractive, and you will continue to experience resistance and repulsion as long as you do. Role modeling your true authenticity empowers and enriches you. It makes you attractive and desirable.

And now that you know who you really are, you have the opportunity to role model your true self and experience authentic, empowered, purposeful living that flows effortlessly.

To the degree that you live and role model your own individual, magnificent Self, you will just naturally do and have what is appropriate for you. And you will have these magnificent results

70

merely by being who you most love to be and doing the things that bring you the greatest sense of joy, satisfaction and fulfillment.

You may ask, "Why was it so important to identify the qualities I love?" Because, they are your Values, Your VALUES are the qualities that you love, the ones that you value. Your God given Soul is comprised of your Values. Your Soul is the source of your core Values.

Role Modeling these authentic Soul Values makes you very attractive, because all of us are attracted to these same noble values. It is by the Values or the vices you express that the world determines who you are. To the degree you express vices instead of virtue, the world will resist you.

But getting on Purpose and expressing your authentic, attractive Values, you will experience your life beginning to soar. Your Values will begin attracting to you all that you can envision and dream in the Vision Exercise in Step 3.

Before proceeding, perhaps during the process of Unfolding Your Personal Purpose, your Priority rankings may have changed as they often do. Return now to Step One to see if yours have changed. If so, write your revised rankings in the next available ranking column.

With re-ranking complete, you will now want to create your Vision Statement in Step 3, "Unfolding Your Personal Vision". Keeping in mind your new, attractive, empowered, purposeful Self, you should create grand visions in each area and achieve them easily.

Step 3: Unfolding Your Personal Vision

Your Personal Vision is your dream of what you would love to HAVE or HAVE ACCOMPLISHED by some specific future time, like in 5 years. When you write down your individual, personal Vision, a special dream of what you want to accomplish in your life, it becomes quite simple to achieve.

You will now identify and write down precisely what your Vision is in each of the eight Key Areas. A Vision that is not written is only a fleeting dream. Without a written Vision, you will be lucky if you achieve even half of what you are capable of. Without a written Vision, dream, or long-range goal, you won't really know which way to go, nor be satisfied that you have ever truly arrived.

This process enables you to envision all eight key areas of your life together so that your Vision will be comprehensive and balanced, as well as supportive of who you are and where you want to go. You don't want to spend your life climbing to the top of the ladder only to find it leaning against the wrong wall.

Your Personal Vision provides a valuable yardstick to evaluate each of your Goals, or future action steps that you may consider. You will be able to measure whether an action is adequate or necessary, or whether it will carry you to or away from your Vision.

Clarifying and writing your Visions (have's) naturally precedes your goal setting. Any Goals (do's) that you set without a clear Vision of where you are going, will automatically be, to some degree, off Purpose and un-empowered. This Visioning process will also be interesting as a source of further self-discovery.

Of equal importance, your eight Vision statements will enable you to accurately communicate where you are planning to go to your family, associates and mentors. They will all be much better informed, and therefore much more helpful, supportive and understanding.

Anything you would love to have, you can have. Write it down now and then think about it. Don't make it up. Listen to your heart. You already know down deep what brings you both satisfaction and fulfillment, what you love.

Be as expansive and grand as is true for you. Know you will not fail. Don't neglect any area. Remember this is your opportunity to design a complete, exciting future, one worth working for and living into.

Don't be like the person who said "I always wanted to be somebody when I grew up. Now that I am grown, I wish I had been more specific."

The following guidelines will help you create your Vision statements. They may not all apply to any single one of the eight key areas. They will, however, assist you in considering what you might want to include in your Vision statement. Remember, be as detailed as possible.

Wherever possible tell who, what, when, where, and how much. Clearly picture the result in your mind and then write it in detail. The more specific your Vision, the more certain your results.

Know too, "If you can't measure it, you can't manage it."

GUIDELINES for Acquisition or Accomplishment

CAREER: Position, Field, Compensation, Job Satisfaction, Advancement, Accomplishment

FAMILY: Spouse, Children, Family Activities, Home, Amenities, Quality of life, Closeness

FINANCIAL: Income, Net Worth, Budget, Cash, Credit Line, Retirement Savings, Investments

73

MENTAL: Mental Growth achievement, Degrees, Knowledge, Skills, Abilities, Languages

PHYSICAL: Health, Appearance, Weight, Fitness, Capability, Exercise Routine, Sports Ability

RELATIONSHIP: Network of Friends, Associates, Colleagues, Mentors, Advisors, Romances

SPIRITUAL: Religious Study, Knowledge, Understanding, Faith, Prayer, Meditation, Gratitude

SERVING: Volunteering, Generosity, Difference made, Giving Back, Support, Contribution

Below, write down what you would love to HAVE achieved, acquired, created, improved, or better related to for each of the eight '5 year Vision Statements.' Write your grandest dream of what you would love to HAVE or HAVE accomplished in five years.   Really go for it. Write it as if it is already accomplished.

1)   In my Career, I would love to HAVE or HAVE accomplished:

2)   With my Family, I would love to HAVE or HAVE accomplished:

3)   Financially, I would love to HAVE or HAVE accomplished:

4)   Mentally, I would love to HAVE or HAVE accomplished:

5)   Physically, I would love to HAVE or HAVE accomplished:

6)   In my Relationships, I would love to HAVE or HAVE accomplished:

7)   Spiritually, I would love to HAVE or HAVE accomplished:

8) In Serving others, I would love to HAVE or HAVE accomplished:

The following sample Personal Vision Statement is included as an abbreviated Example only. Your Vision statement will naturally be quite different and more detailed and complete.

EXAMPLE: My Personal Vision in five years is to HAVE accomplished:

1.   Mentally, to have become proficient in internet commerce, Twitter, Face Book, Learned Spanish and read three books on business each year.

2.   Spiritually, to have written a treatise on the practical understanding of man's expanded possibilities as the 'likeness of God' and published it.

3.   With my Family, to be experiencing on-going warm, loving, intimate, fun relationship with my wife, children and grandchildren, held an annual reunion, and bought a 3,000 sq. ft. home with a pool in Tanglewood.

4.   Physically, to have maintained good health, vitality, agility and endurance; walked one mile daily, played tennis twice weekly and skied annually.

5.   In my Career, to own my own engineering consulting business with ten employees doing over $3 million per year, with all my employees having significant satisfaction, fun, fulfillment and prosperity.

6.   In my Relationships, have a happy, mutually contributing relationship with 20 friends through tennis, bridge, church and club parties, with 3 activities/week.

7.   Financially, to have maintained a sense of financial freedom, prosperity, security and generosity, and maintained a balanced portfolio with personal net worth of $ _____ and an annual income of $ _____ .

8.   Serving, to have developed an improved Personal Purpose Process and have it in use by one thousand students annually, enabling them to create vastly more purposeful, productive, fulfilling and joyous lives. Be actively mentoring two college students and five Prison Entrepreneurship Program graduates.

Now, in light of the above Example, review your Personal Vision statements and if any of them need revising, rewrite them on the next page. Continue to revise them until they feel right for you now but expect to modify them frequently in the coming year.

Continue to be bold, grand and inspiring. Create an exciting Vision worth really going for. But most of all, be detailed and specific.

My Personal Vision in 5 years is to HAVE or HAVE accomplished the following:

1) In my Career, I would love to HAVE or HAVE accomplished:

2) With my family, I would love to HAVE or HAVE accomplished:

3) Financially, I would love to HAVE or HAVE accomplished:

4) Mentally, I would love to HAVE or HAVE accomplished:

5) Physically, I would love to HAVE or HAVE accomplished:

6) In my Relationships, I would love to HAVE or HAVE accomplished:

7) Spiritually, I would love to HAVE or HAVE accomplished:

8) In Serving others, I would love to HAVE or HAVE accomplished:

Are these clearly statements of what you really would love to HAVE ACCOMPLISHED

in 5 years? If so, then return to Step One and see if in the process of unfolding your personal Visions, your priority rankings have changed. If they have, re-rank each facet, writing your revised rankings into the next available ranking column. With this complete, you may now go on to Step 4, "Choosing Your Personal Goals."

STEP 4: CHOOSING YOUR PERSONAL GOALS

Your Personal Goals are the action steps you will take (DO) within one year toward achieving each of your eight Five Year Visions. Examine each Vision and write exactly what you will love to DO in the next year toward achieving each one.

Write at least one goal for each Vision. Stretch yourself, assume you can't possibly fail. Be bold and SPECIFIC as to who, what when, and how much. Write exactly what you must do over the next year to progress appropriately toward your Vision and be comfortably "on Purpose" in doing it.

By choosing the right goals, you will be able to achieve them and complete your Five Year Visions on time, and with success and satisfaction.

My 20__ Personal Goals are:

1)   In my Career I would love to (DO)

2)   With my Family I would love to (DO)

3)   Financially, I would love to (DO)

4)   Mentally, I would love to (DO)

5)   Physically, I would love to (DO)

6)   In my Relationships, I would love to (DO)

7)   Spiritually, I would love to (DO)

8)   In Serving others, I would love to (DO)

You may find that your task for the next year looks difficult, however, if your Visions are exciting, don't go back and water them down, watch for ideas to enable them to quickly appear. Having now created your eight "love to DO" Personal Goals for the coming year, be sure your Goals specifically support each of your eight Vision statements.

Review each Goal to see that it carries you appropriately and aggressively toward each Vision. Also, review the example below. If changes seem necessary, rewrite your revised Goals into the blanks below.

EXAMPLE: My Personal Goals for year 20__ are:

1.   Mentally: take one computer course and read three books on improving business skills.

2.   Spiritually: to write an outline and draft treatise on "Expanding man's Godlike potential."

3.   With my Family: to spend two hours of quality time daily with my wife, visit each of my out of state children twice and arrange a family reunion this year. Start our house search.

4.   Physically: walk a mile daily, play tennis twice a week and ski one week this year.

5.   Career: Plan and open my engineering consulting practice with two employees.

6.   In my Relationships: Play bridge, tennis and have dinner with friends each week.

7.   Financially: Sell $ _____ worth of my RE inventory and arrange my portfolio to securely produce a 5% return and budget household expenses to $_____ this year.

8.   Serving: Begin using the Personal Purpose Process in one prison and add one school this year and make it available on a web site. Continue entrepreneurship mentoring with seven mentees this year.

Now it's your turn..........

My 20__ Personal Goals are:

1) In my Career I would love to (DO)

2) With my Family I would love to (DO)

3) Financially, I would love to (DO)

4) Mentally, I would love to (DO)

5) Physically, I would love to (DO)

6) In my Relationships, I would love to (DO)

7) Spiritually, I would love to (DO)

8) In Serving others, I would love to (DO)

After finalizing Your Personal Goals, return to Step 1 a final time and if changes are necessary, write your revised rankings in the next available column.

Congratulations!!!

You have now completed a personal plan that fully assures you of a successful, well rounded life in all eight areas if it is kept current and faithfully followed.

If you are now satisfied with your answers to Sections 1 through 4, type a Summary on a word processor and both print it out, and save the file for up-dating later. (See the next page for a sample Summary format.) Your Personal Purpose Process will continue to progress and develop, perhaps for years.

It is important to go back and up-date your Summary regularly or you will begin to dismiss the value of it because some part is obsolete. Also, give a printed copy to one person, perhaps your mentor or your significant other, and get their feed-back. If you then choose to make changes, alter the original file and again print it out.

Ask another friend to critique it. From their comments, you may notice areas that you would like to improve, but don't allow them to dampen your dreams. Reread it for several days making any updates needed.

When your goals settle down, then go to work. It may help to divide some goals into several pieces and schedule a date for achieving each portion throughout the year.

The Personal Purpose Process has unbelievable power if you keep a copy handy to remind you of the exciting Visions you are working toward. Be sure to timely execute each step of your Goals as scheduled.

As was previously mentioned, you will benefit from every part of the Personal Purpose, and you will benefit even more when you use it to communicate to those around you. The more they know about who you are and where you are going, the more they can help you. Providence always helps a person who is committed to where he/she is going.

Monte Pendleton

mpendleton@silverfox.org

www.thepersonalpurpose.com

<<< S A M P L E >>>

My Personal Purpose Summary

January 1, 20__

My final Priority rankings:

Career # 8   Family # 2   Financial # 3   Mental # 4   Physical # 5
Relationships # 7   Spiritual # 1   Serving # 6

Values I Love to Express with my:

FAMILY: Love, Joy, Caring, Support, Intimacy, Kindness, Purity, Unity, Harmony, Thoughtfulness, Consideration

FINANCE: Abundance, Security, Wisdom, Trustworthiness, Freedom, Comfort, Satisfaction, Blessing, Value, Good

SPIRITUAL: Faith, Adoration, Gratitude, Humility, Forgiveness, Grace, Understanding, Growth, Loyalty, Trust, Peace

PHYSICAL: Perfection, Health, Beauty, Strength, Vitality, Capability, Action, Endurance, Energy, Productivity

MENTAL: Alertness, Intelligence, Wisdom, Vision, Focus, Order, Balance, Knowledge, Guidance, Memory, Purpose

SOCIAL: Friendship, Happiness, Fun, Loyalty, Sharing, Blessing, Rewarding, Fulfillment, Purposeful, Attraction

SERVICE: Contribution, Support, Benevolence, Caring, Blessing, Serving, Generosity, Giving, Benefitting, Mentoring

CAREER: Leadership, Organization, Empowerment, Resourceful, Honesty, Integrity, Success, Reward, Satisfaction

My Personal Purpose is to be a role model of Love, Caring, Abundance, Satisfaction, Understanding, Trust, Health, Productivity, Wisdom, Memory, Happiness, Friendship, Blessing, Support, Empowerment, Leadership and Purpose, which will Inspire, Empower, Bless and Benefit my Family, Friends, Mentees and Associates.

My Personal Vision in five years is to HAVE accomplished: (These are condensed.)

1.	Mentally: Become proficient in internet commerce, Twitter, Face Book, Learned Spanish and read three books on business each year.

2.	Spiritually: To have written a treatise on the practical understanding of man's expanded possibilities as the 'likeness of God' and published it.

3.	With my Family: Be experiencing on-going warm, loving, intimate, fun relationship with my wife, children and grand children, held an annual reunion, and bought a 3,000 sq. ft. home with a pool in Tanglewood.

4.	Physically: Have maintained good health, vitality, agility and endurance; walked one mile daily, played tennis twice weekly and skied annually.

5.   In my Career: Own my own engineering consulting business with ten employees doing over $3 million per year, with all my employees having significant satisfaction, fun, fulfillment and prosperity.

6.   Relationship: Have a happy, mutually contributing relationship with 20 friends through tennis, bridge, church and club parties, with 3 activities/week.

7.   Financially: Have maintained a sense of financial freedom, prosperity, security and generosity, and maintained a balanced portfolio with personal net worth of

$ _____ and an annual income of $ _____.

8.   Serving: Have developed an improved Personal Purpose Process and have it in use by one thousand students annually, enabling them to create vastly more purposeful, productive, fulfilling and joyous lives. Be actively mentoring two UH students and five Prison Entrepreneurship Program graduates.

EXAMPLE: My Personal Goals for year 20__ are:

   1.   Mentally: Take one computer course and read three books on improving business skills.

2.   Spiritually: Write an outline and draft treatise on "Expanding man's Godlike potential."

3.   With my Family: Spend two hours of quality time daily with my wife, visit each of my out of state children twice and arrange a family reunion this year. Start our house search.

4.   Physically: walk a mile daily, play tennis twice a week and ski one week this year.

5.   In my Career: Plan and open my engineering consulting practice with two employees.

6.	In my Relationships: Play bridge, tennis and have dinner with friends each week.

7.	Financially: Sell $ _____ worth of my RE inventory and arrange my portfolio to securely produce a 5% return and budget household expenses to $_____ this year.

8.	Serving: Begin using the Personal Purpose Process in one prison and add one school this year and make it available on a web site. Continue entrepreneurship mentoring with seven mentees this year.

BONUS #2 LinkedIn

LinkedIn has been around over 15 years (yes, it's hard to believe). It has become, by far, the most prolific platform for people in the work world. All the other social media platforms combined cannot surpass the power and vision that LinkedIn has for job seekers.

I've been on the system since 2005. I taught the first workshop on LinkedIn held in the greater Houston area. My work in coaching and teaching LinkedIn has been featured in Fortune magazine.

As part of the work we did at Jobs Ministry Southwest, we became pioneers for teaching the merits, tips and tricks of powering through on LinkedIn. I originally boiled down into a program I titled "12.5 Ways to get Ahead on LinkedIn". As the name implies, here are the original thoughts on effectively using LinkedIn.

Start by thinking about a "sales minded approach" for your job search. You are a product and a brand that must be "sold" to the prospective company and the hiring manager. Your time, your skills, and your services need to be explained as a solution to a company's need. (See Value Proposition in STRIVE)

So, every time you decide to put information out on the Internet:

- Build a professional Internet presence in the "Profile"
- Establish your "brand"
- Highlight accomplishments
- Offer solutions
- Attract and grow an effective network
- Perform high powered market intelligence
- Research facts and stats
- Gather recommendations and opinions
- Prepare for Interviews

Step 1. Build a Great Profile – then get the Word Out

Use all the tools and tricks inside LinkedIn to build a great profile. However, you should stay away from the traditional Resume mindset in building your profile. Instead, tell a story about what you have to offer.

Use the **status updates** broadcast to your entire network. Once someone adds you as a contact, every status update you make will be sent to those contacts.

However, this is NOT Twitter or Facebook. Keep the updates professional and focused on your work.

- LinkedIn sends network updates with each change
  - Don't over-do it
  - Keep it fresh
- Make alerts about events where you might be "appearing"
- Share insights on hot topics; limited space though
- Watch your written communication

Step 2. Get Connected

Look through your current contact list and decide who you want to add to your LinkedIn connections. You can manually load the connection invitation information or use the upload features to connect. LinkedIn can read your current contacts from Outlook or any other contact management software you might use.

When you want to send someone an invitation to connect, DO NOT settle for the built-in template. Write a personal message to your contacts. Make the person believe you are sincere about wanting to make the connection.

Watch your email etiquette. Respond promptly.

Be sure you are making good contacts. Creating a big email blast to ask for connections may result in some of your invitations being rejected.

NOTE: LinkedIn will keep score on the number of times your invitations to connect get rejected (i.e. the recipient/invitee declines your request). Five (5) or more rejects and your account will be frozen.

Stay in touch with your contacts; follow-up with people on a regular basis.

Step 3. Ask for Recommendations

Use your connections to ask for recommendations. You will get to review the recommendation before you post it. You can even reject the writing if you choose.

This is a great place to get former bosses and colleagues to comment. Make it credible though. Remember, you are building a brand value. Look for ways to have others tell parts of your story.

Ask for this feedback by using the request for recommendation that LinkedIn provides. It is a good, somewhat formalized process to send requests, receive results, review the writing, and then post to your profile.

People who agree to write something for you might come back and ask for reciprocal recommendations (that means you endorse them too). That's OK. Pay it forward.

Step 4. Work on Keywords

Every industry has a wealth of keywords (formerly known as "buzz words"). These are terms, names, and descriptions of things that are pertinent to what you should know.

Use them ALOT. Put them in your text info on your profile. If you don't finish covering the list in your profile, build a KEYWORD section at the end.

Keywords get scanned and indexed by the LinkedIn software. This is what recruiters and hiring managers use to screen people.

Make your brand rich with keywords. Build a good list by reviewing job descriptions that "fit" the things you want to do. If you need to, use tools like Google for finding the right keywords. Build a solid list that represents who you are and what you know. This can add brand value for you.

Step 5. Print the Marketing Handout

There is a small Adobe™ icon on your profile page. Once you have completed all of your profile, try clicking this button.

You will be AMAZED at the document this creates for you. Use it as a handout when you are networking in person. Or save it to send to contacts once you begin a discussion about your job search/goals.

Step 6. Search for Target Companies

LinkedIn has some great data about participating companies. Company data can be found for a large, growing number of these. Click the "Companies" tab from the LinkedIn Home page.

Use whatever criteria you choose. Then scroll through all of the information.

- Find other possible contacts
- Get lists of officers
- Find data about the companies (e.g. sales, industry stats, products, other buzz)
- Use this information to prepare for meetings and interviews
- Be prepared to discuss topics and insights with interviewers
- Look at the similar companies listed
- Review the information about the competition

Step 7. Ask for Insights

Reach out to your contacts.

- Use network contacts to ask for opinions about target companies
- Ask "who do you know"
- Get the informal organization structure
- Learn about corporate culture
- Rely on former employees, not necessarily current ones
- Ask polite, but specific questions
- Can you tell me something about....?

Step 8. Search LinkedIn Events

LinkedIn members can post upcoming events. Use the search capabilities to browse for events that may be covering ideas and interests from your targets.

If you need more ideas about where to network in person, search these events. Look for new ideas. Think outside of your box.

Look for names of people with whom you want to connect. See what events they attend.

When all else fails, check out other topics, industries, and ideas.

Create your own event. This may be a very bold move. If you do not see an event you that interests you, get with some friends and associates to schedule your own event. Local restaurants usually have meeting rooms that can be reserved for very little cost.

Step 9. Join LinkedIn Groups

Use the Groups to meet other people of like mind. LinkedIn groups can be created by anyone. If you cannot find a group, create your own, then invite people to join.

Browse the Group Directory to find groups you may be interested in joining, then do it.

- Monitor group discussions and participate in them
- Make comments
- Get recognized
- Look for people with whom you can make a direct connection, then send the invitation to connect

Step10. Build Value with Answers

Use the Questions and Answers section to respond to questions. Show readers your expertise by writing good answers to the many questions that are posted.

LinkedIn allows people to ask questions. These can cover anything. Show people what you know by answering some of the many questions that are asked. Your ideas may catch someone's attention.

If the person asking the question decides yours is the best answer, you get recognition. Your profile will show the results of the ratings for your answers.

This is a great way to be recognized by third party sources as an expert in your field.

Step 11. Make Referrals

LinkedIn is still all about social networking. Don't forget that. Networking is simply meeting new people who might be able to direct you to another connection (another person); and so on, and so on.

It is about building high trust relationships where each person gets comfortable referring the other person. In its simplest form, it is one-on-one relationship building.

One colleague once asked "can we ever have enough GOOD people in our network"? The obvious answer is NO!

Work your network and help other people connect. The key rule of networking is to pay-it-forward; give before getting.

Do this same thing on LinkedIn. When you connect with someone new, do not forget about offering suggestions about other people they might be interested in meeting. These unsolicited introductions given to a new contact can help you gain a better reputation as someone available and willing to help.

- Cherish the contacts, respect people's privacy
- Respect people's time and confidence
- Help make things grow

Step 12. Use the LinkedIn Applications

LinkedIn applications ("apps") are sometimes called "widgets". These are tools that can be added to your profile page. The best uses of the apps are to expand the content you share on LinkedIn.

Here are some examples:

- You can share files and folders of work product you are willing to demonstrate
- PowerPoint presentations you have written
- Spreadsheet models
- White papers you have published
- Academic papers, articles
- Blog pages you write and update
- Photo albums of professional projects (resist the temptation to use family or personal photos)

By presenting these materials, you are adding to your brand value and building a bigger story for people wanting to know you.

Step 12.5: Use Your Profile Link EVERYWHERE

As you build your profile, there is a web link that is created. It looks something like:

http://www.LinkedIn.com/in/yourname

It is found in the settings of your profile page. If you do not like the default name it gives you, you can try editing it. However, LinkedIn has final say since this link becomes an actual web address that must be truly unique. That means you cannot copy someone else's name and link if you like theirs better.

Use it everywhere you post your name: business cards, resumes, emails, handouts. Be sure people know you are on LinkedIn. Draw traffic to your LinkedIn page.

BONUS POINTS

Here are a few final tips that have come out of the live seminars.

1.   Should I use a photo or not? Your personal appearance is an inevitable fact of life. Hiding behind a LinkedIn profile without a good photo is not going to help in the long run. Use a simple head and shoulders shot.

Get it done with a good digital camera. DO NOT use a family picture with your spouse, kids, or your dog nearby. This is your professional brand image, remember?

2.   What about my email address? Be sure your email address is also a good professional representation of your brand.

FuzzyBunny@blahblah.com does not make the right impression. Use one of the many email providers who offer free service like Google (gmail) or Yahoo. The domain name is not as significant as the prefix (your name).

3.   What if someone does not respond to my invitation to connect? Likely you have not yet established enough of a relationship for them to agree to respond. First do some more work in building the actual relationship. Your LinkedIn contacts should represent real, live connections you have with people.

BIBLIOGRAPHY

Gillis, R. (2010). *Job!* Houston, TX, USA.

Pendleton, M. (2013). Co-Founder, SIlver Fox Advisors. Houston, Texas.

OTHER WORKS BY DOUG THORPE

"The Uncommon Commodity: The Common Sense Guide for New Managers", available on Amazon, Kindle and theuncommoncommodity.com

"Launch a Great Business: Top 10 Ways to Make Your Company Soar", available on Amazon

"8 Ways to Grow Your Business and Increase Profits", available on Amazon and Kindle

"Finding Your Edge: How to Create Financial Freedom Through Marketing Your Business", available on Amazon and Kindle

Visit Doug at https://DougThorpe.com for articles from his highly successful "Leadership Powered by Common Sense."

Download the podcasts at podcasts.dougthorpe.com

www.ingramcontent.com/pod-product-compliance
Lightning Source LLC
Chambersburg PA
CBHW022123280326
41933CB00007B/513